CULTIVATE YOUR **CORE** TALENT

Profit from Your Natural Ability in Eight Simple Steps

CULTIVATE YOUR **CORE** TALENT

Profit from Your Natural Ability in Eight Simple Steps

REKESHA PITTMAN

GET WRITE PUBLISHING

CULTIVATE YOUR CORE TALENT

Profit from Your Natural Ability in Eight Simple Steps

ISBN: 979-8-9897768-2-5

The EAST Formula
2770 Main Street - Suite 97
Frisco, TX 75034

Printed in the United States of America.

CONTENTS

IDENTIFY YOUR CORE TALENT

I am going to share a key concept that will revolutionize your life; **identify your core talent**. I believe that every person has a core talent. It is your gift; something innate within that you can do naturally. Your core talent is the *one* skill or ability that is easy for you and is often requested by others. You can never run out of it, and you might grow to resent it if everyone else is benefiting from it except you.

People repeat sayings like, "Pursue your passion and the money will follow." Guess what? Sometimes you can burn out or your passions can change. You can have a passion that will keep you in poverty. I've been there and I've experienced it.

If more people operated through their core talent, I think that they would have more money. People will tell you that if you discover your purpose, then everything will be clear. I believe that maybe we don't have one single thing we're supposed to do for the rest of our lives. Many people are confused and frustrated right now because they cannot figure out what their purpose is. Your core talent is evident. Now, use it.

So, how can you discover what your core talent is? Here's a clue… It's something that people probably ask you for all the time. You cannot escape or deny it. Everywhere you go, whether in the workplace, in the marketplace, in the educational sector, or in your local community, people ask you for it. Also, they are happy to receive it from you.

When I was an employee, it didn't matter what my job title indicated. I was always the person that my coworkers would approach with questions. They wanted me to teach and train them to do multiple things.

When I worked as a social worker, my supervisor would take my caseload from me and ask me to train the entire staff. When I was in human resources, it was the same thing; I was asked to be a trainer.

I discovered that I could teach and train at a master level that simplified information and concepts for people to easily understand. Not only could they understand me clearly, but they were also able to implement my teaching and training methods to produce real world results.

My core talent is teaching and training. When I write books, they serve as teaching and training tools. As a professional speaker, I am teaching and training. When I offer online sessions, I am teaching and training. Whenever I host events, I am still teaching and training.

The thing that feeds me, and the thing that causes cash to flow my way, is my core talent: teaching and training. Yours may be something else. Are you always asked to cook by family, friends, and associates? Your core talent may be cooking. Do you see where I'm going with this?

To clarify this for yourself, take time to self-reflect or ask people who know you very well what they think you do expertly. After this, I believe that you will discover a clue or be able to identify your core talent precisely.

Your core talent may also be something that you keep receiving as an assignment. You do not volunteer for it. You do not ask for it, but everywhere you go, you end up with that task.

In almost every personal and professional environment, I ended up with a leadership position that I didn't ask for. Why? Because I can teach and train at a high level. When you help people, they are more likely to keep following you.

What is it that keeps "assigning" itself to you? This is a clue to discovering your core talent. Maybe you just need just a little more information to make it work. Take some time to identify your core talent and you will get closer to increased cash flow.

TURN YOUR TALENT INTO TREASURE

Once you identify your core talent, you can turn that talent into treasure. To do this, you're going to need to be able to recognize value. Then, you can create income with it.

I had to learn how to recognize my own value. Because some things come naturally to me, it is my instinct to share it with others or give it away. I would say things like, "Oh, you don't have to pay me for that… we're friends" or "It's not a problem." I was giving away something that I could have exchanged for money.

I have volunteered for events that the host should have hired a professional to work. They were capitalizing on my core talent before I was able to recognize what I was giving away. In essence, I was profitable for them while robbing myself. I'm not saying that it's wrong to volunteer; it's just not smart to continue letting people take advantage of you and pocket the profits.

What is the value that you can place on your core talent to be able to exchange it for payment? Here's one way that you're going to be able to recognize value and establish healthy boundaries around your talent: set limits on your volunteerism! Some of us have been conditioned to volunteer, do the right thing, or to serve. We have this mentality that what we do naturally should be a free service. A wise woman taught me to put an end date on my volunteerism assignments.

If there are any assignments that you have accepted and you are volunteering more than you are benefiting, then you need to put an end date on that assignment. I do believe in serving others. I do believe that you should perform benevolent acts. However, because some of us have taken responsibility for helping others without an end date, we don't have room to grow a business, we don't have time to market a business, and we don't have enough focus to be able to put good systems in place.

Stop allowing yourself to be overwhelmed with volunteer activities that are not allowing your core talent to convert into treasure.

From now on, set an end date when you agree to volunteer. If someone asks you to volunteer, you can say, "I can do this for 30 days," or, "I can do this for one project only." You're going to have to focus if you expect to turn your talents into treasure.

Nothing is free. Everything has a cost. Some of us are paying people to enjoy the things we offer, like freebies or giveaways. Count the cost.

Over a decade ago, I offered my first publishing course for $99.00. It ran for seven weeks, and my clients were successful. This was well before course creation software became popular. I was happy at the time to add a few hundred dollars to my income.

After my concept was proven, I expanded that material into a 12-month interactive course. I added value by incorporating pre-recorded video, live video training, and scheduled Q&A sessions. At the end of the program, each author attended a live ceremony with a copy of their book in hand for proof. It became my first 6-figure offer.

Since then, I have developed a range of programs, including both low-ticket and high-ticket offers. While I refuse to make false promises to my clients, I teach them my systems that have worked for many years to provide the equivalent of a salary for me, even through my leanest years.

Start somewhere. If you already have proven experience, find a way to increase the value of what you have to offer and allow yourself an opportunity to build a legitimate business based on what you can do naturally. If you have a hard time determining what to charge, study the success stories in your industry.

Remember that everything has a value. Did it cost you time? Did it cost you money? Did it cost you effort? Did it cost you an opportunity? Giving away too much time or overbooking your calendar can cause you to miss out on things that would have opened new doors of opportunity. Discover what works for you and work it.

Even if you decide to give something away, assign a monetary value to what you're sharing. This is one of the methods taught for lead generation. It costs you something to share what you have with others. This will help you to not feel guilty when it's time to send an invoice, quote that price, make a pitch, and close the deal. Turn your talents into treasure!

MONETIZE YOUR CORE TALENT

Based on your core talent, you should be able to develop a product or service. For instance, I am a master teacher and systematic trainer. My services include professional consulting for book publishing, online courses, group coaching, strategy sessions, and hosting VIP days. I'm a problem solver. I can teach and train in ways that people understand clearly.

What about products? As an author, I have multiple books that I can sell online and at appearances. I also offer digital downloads and videos with instant viewing access. In addition to my services, there's something tangible that someone can purchase, and I can deliver. My products are designed to help them reach a certain goal or solve a specific problem they are encountering.

When you identify your core talent, make a list of products and services you can create. You don't have to offer the entire menu at the same time. Write down any potential products and/or services that you would be able to market based on your core talent.

Determine if you have a service and how you would provide it. From that service, you can develop products that complement your offer. These will be tangible items that you're going to sell, ship, or deliver.

You will need proper systems to manage the services offered. If you expect to be compensated for your talents, you must be willing to invest in them yourself. Although you don't have to have perfect systems in place to offer your services, a basic website, sales page, or online form should help to capture the information you need to follow up with any prospects.

In general, people are more willing to enter their credit card information in places that feel secure. I always ask people that I train questions like, "Do you look like a good investment? Do you look like a vault? Do you look like a safe place for my money?" How you handle transactions is a direct reflection of how you "look" in the eyes of others.

Professional graphics are also good tools to use to capture the attention of your ideal audience and turn your talents into treasure. Poorly designed flyers, pixelated pictures, and disjointed font choices can hinder your chances and make you look like a novice. Having screenshots of excellent design will help guide you and your team of experts and eliminate some of the guesswork. Your brand matters.

Let's review items versus information. When you stream on social media, share a training video, or post content online, that's information. Personally, I do not charge for sharing information, but I *do* get paid well for implementation! Providing information is how I get people to buy my products and services.

If you want people to know that you're an expert, you're going to have to become a source of helpful information. You may have to answer common questions about your core talent. You may post short videos that allow people to access your expertise and see your core talent at work.

I like to go live via video so that I can re-purpose my content in many ways to attract eyes to my talent. I can post clips of my longer videos on my profile, share highlights in stories, create reels for social media, or add them to my website as a commercial. Because I engage with my audience when I am live, I can capture their comments and share those as social media content.

To enhance the quality of my videos, I make sure to have a clear camera, sufficient lighting, good sound, and a suitable background. The process does not have to be perfect. Some of my most popular videos are of me walking around outside. The key to proving your expertise or offering a product is consistency.

When you're thinking about products, will you offer printed materials? Merchandise? Branded items? Will your products have images, quotes, or catchphrases connected to your industry printed on them? You can sell products related to your core talent that are profitable.

Even though all my product lines weren't successful, each of them provided a lesson that I needed to improve my strategy. When I started producing shirts, I did not realize that there was a fashion forecast every year. In advance, manufacturers were aware of which Pantone colors would be used in each season and stocked their shelves accordingly. After I signed up for fashion design courses and attended industry fabric shows, I realized why I had poor sales in some colors and sold out of others.

I embraced my creativity and wasn't afraid to try. After spending countless hours buying t-shirt blanks, transfers, labels, and pressing the shirts in my living room, I found a factory that could manufacture them for about half of what I was paying for materials. They used their bulk buying power to pass on the savings to my business. I didn't even count my labor costs, so I was winning! Since I understood the process of creating the shirts myself, I knew what to ask for from the manufacturer.

The bonus for finding a manufacturer was that they provided much more than t-shirt production. I had options to expand my line to jackets, hoodies, tumblers, bags, and even custom items. My core talent was not assembling shirts in the heat or staying up all night to press them. I was wasting time and money until I reassigned that role to the experts.

If you want to turn your talents into treasure, it's not going to happen magically. Many people don't like to sell things because there is an element of rejection. What's more important to you? Fear or finances? And really, what are you afraid of?

There are people, books, conferences, and connections that have the exact information you need. You must be willing to explore these options by escaping from your comfort zone and attending conferences, networking events, and meetings that will grant you the freedom to partner with others and enhance your talent. Instead of asking too many questions initially, I listen first and then know who to talk to in a room based on their introduction or expertise.

Even if you are already making money, what is keeping you from reaching the next level of achievement that you desire? What is it that you still need to learn? What systems, methods, teams, or contacts do you need to succeed?

Your talents are worth treasure. You're going to have to make up your mind that this is what you want. You're going to have to accept that you are worthy of wealth based on your own skills. Then, get ready to make money while you make moves.

OFFER YOUR CORE TALENT

The next thing that you're going to have to do is deal with your mentality about your talent and how much money you have the potential to make. Confront any insecurities that you may have about your distinct talent. Then, decide what it would take financially to free yourself from allowing others to profit more from your talents than you have.

If you want to sail through selling, learn some key tactics by reading books, attending educational sessions, or completing courses. Create a unique selling proposition or pitch based on current methods. Maybe the way that you are presenting your offer doesn't lead to a sale. Maybe you're downplaying yourself, like many people do. When you receive a compliment, don't say, "Oh, it's not that big of a deal…" Refuse to diminish your talents. Don't downplay what you do.

Find the right words to use, even if that means that you find them somewhere else.

You may have to hire a copywriter. Maybe you will need to build a team around your strategy to produce results and introduce your offer in a way that helps you exchange that talent for treasure. You are your primary investor, so be prepared to pay to play.

As you succeed, it is also helpful to gather testimonials. If there is anybody who has received services or goods from you and they are satisfied with what they've experienced, be sure to get a testimonial. I collect written testimonials on my website or via social media, and video testimonials on my phone or personally during events.

Share testimonials on your platforms and sales pages. It is a good practice to request permission to share them. This will help others see proof of your work and convince them that your talent is worth an investment.

Remain consistent. Don't merely show up occasionally and believe that the cash register (virtual or physical) is going to keep ringing. Create a solid marketing plan and content calendar. Schedule your posts in advance, if needed. Showcase your brand, business, products, ideas, and offers on a regular basis.

Here is an evaluation that I perform often: If I visit your social media platforms, will I be able to confirm your legitimacy? Will I be able to verify you as an expert in your field? Can I establish that you are a true person of business? Would I be able to find that you are serious and committed to turning your talents into treasure?

If you claim to be in business, you must consistently prove that you can be trusted to show up for the job. What does your online presence reveal about you? It's time to be honest and not delusional.

Some people wonder why others are not supporting them. Hardly anyone is investing in them. They're not buying from them. It's because they don't believe them! Make sure that we can believe you.

BRAND YOUR CORE TALENT

Branding can be a difficult concept to grasp unless you are clear about your offer. Beyond a logo, tagline, colors, fonts, and icons, a brand is what is "burned" into the minds of people when (and after) they experience you, your service, your product, your packaging, your website, your team, your location … get the picture?

Your core talent must become part of your lifestyle. So, live your brand. There are enough imposters online selling to suckers. Create a legacy that you can be proud of.

My brand demanded my participation. When I first started as an entrepreneur, excellence was my primary focus. Because of that approach, people literally insisted that I create a method for them to pay me to teach and train them. As a result, I have had the opportunity to assist over 1,000 authors worldwide in addition to having founded several brands and profitable enterprises. I am an entrepreneur, author, speaker, and trainer. Everything that I do backs up that claim.

If people perceive that you are all over the place or inconsistent, you will need to clean up your brand. This may mean taking a hard look at your online presence. You may have to have a few hard conversations and make some adjustments to your character, habits, or personality. Otherwise, some people may devalue the talent you have. Refuse to excuse the unnecessary fumbles and work to have a better grasp on your personal and business brands. Decide to become serious about it right now.

Abandon the inaccurate mentality that your social media presence is a personal page or a private hideaway. The companies that created those platforms are making a lot of money by using your name to drive people to their sites, and you can, too. I'm not telling you not to let your personality shine online; however, when people search your name or business to vet you, they are looking to see if you are really about that life. Be about it!

CASH IN ON YOUR CORE TALENT

If you want to turn your talents into treasure, set a money goal. One year, I put 100 bright sticky notes all over my wall where I would see them while working daily at my desk. For each square, I claimed a financial goal of $1,000. Every time I earned $1,000 using my core talents, I would write it boldly on a sticky note until I saw that wall fill up.

What is your cash flow goal? Refuse to aim too low or doubt yourself. You do not have to be overly ambitious. You may decide to make an additional $1,000 per month. How much is that per week? Only $250? That's absolutely achievable! Figure out how to create an offer based on your core talent that will generate $250 weekly: it's as easy as that! Continue to do the math and increase your goals exponentially as a result.

The more money you command, and the income you demand, will be linked to the quality of your offer. Some people may find it easier to sell products and services that other people create. Eventually, these types become disenchanted because working only for the sake of money can create feelings of misalignment. When you earn money by creating success through your natural skills, it's easier to stay committed for long periods of time.

To stay focused, create a visual tool to display. I used to write down my plans and goals on paper. Eventually, I graduated to creating detailed vision boards. What I can say is that I am seeing my visual creativity become my reality!

Some people make vision boards, some people track numbers, others may have a daily sales quota. Whatever you decide, select a visual tracking method for your money goal and make sure to put it in a location that will serve as a daily reminder. If you are truly serious, perform a monthly assessment on yourself to make sure that you are not just dreaming, but doing.

Track the progress of turning your talents into treasure. Every time that you have zero dollars in the sales column for that day, it indicates that there's something more that you need to offer. This may mean more marketing, a different strategy, or a clearly defined audience. Daily tracking gives you enough information to make changes faster.

As part of my development system for emerging entrepreneurs, I created a tracking tool called "The Money Magnet: Success Tracker." I use it to record exactly how much money I bring in for the day. Writing it down makes me deal with reality. If the amount is zero, it's because I didn't send an email, I didn't send a text message, I didn't share a video, I didn't have a funnel, I didn't have a strategy, and I missed a moment. When I market, I make money. We won't need as many money miracles when we have the right methods.

You are going to have to be focused and do the work if you want to turn your talents into treasure. Strategic focus and effort will result in paydays. Your biggest limitation is your own resistance. Next, let's review a few systems that may work for you to cash in on your core talent.

SHARE YOUR CORE TALENT

Being present online is not enough. Show up where your people are most likely to gather and interact with your content. I always say to those with empty nets, "Go where the fish are." If you want to increase your chances of catching fish, you must go to the place where they are plentiful.

Is your ideal community on Instagram? Are they scrolling on Facebook? Are they posting on LinkedIn? Are they on another platform? Where do your best clients linger? Once you know the answer, show up there on a regular basis and learn how to use the different tools available. Whether you use videos, images, graphics, links, stories, reels, podcasts, posts, or audio recordings—find out what your people are responding to and give it to them often.

If you share something and notice that it doesn't get a lot of engagement, use the experience as feedback and do less of that.

When you post online and multiple people respond, that may be the type of content that will work better for your brand. As you offer value, people will keep looking at your pages to see what you're going to share with them. When you do make an offer, you'll already have eyes on your page and that will help to turn your talents into treasure.

No matter what some people claim, you still need an active email list that you are cultivating. This does not mean that you load contacts into your Gmail or add them to the list because you received their business card. There are SPAM laws to protect people, so be sure to use an email service provider to collect contact information or data.

As a business enhancement, I invest in a system that collects names, email addresses, and phone numbers so that I can send emails, text messages, and make phone calls from the same platform. I can see who opened emails, completed requests for information, and my sales reports. As you grow, get systems that will help your money grow as well.

Communicate effectively with your ideal contacts. Your exchange doesn't always have to be for a sale. There are several services that will allow you to connect with people who want to stay informed via a texting service that does not originate from your personal phone. You can automate communications, offer digital downloads, share links, provide exclusive access, or offer discount codes in addition to much more.

I've collected data through many avenues. I can have people scan a QR code online or in-person to receive a digital download, complimentary training, schedule a video meeting, or sign up for a mailing list. You must use the proper service to give people the ability to unsubscribe or opt out. I don't add people just because I have access to their contact info. I include people who are more likely to need my products or services.

Over the years, I have had very few people unsubscribe from my text marketing campaigns because I do not bombard them every single day; however, it does work. This is largely because texting has a better delivery rate than sending emails alone. If I have both a phone number and an email for the same person, I try to alternate the days that I email and text the same list. Be creative and offer more value than sales pitches.

You will need to advertise and spread the news, however you choose to communicate.

It can be through word of mouth, video, creative content, an advertising campaign, marketing materials, or another innovative strategy. You should have no problem sharing your core talent, creating consistent revenue, and generating money as a result. Whatever you do, you're going to have to include some money with your talent and invest in yourself.

MANAGE YOUR CORE TALENT

There are going to be some basic systems that you're going to need to properly collect and track your earnings. You don't have to have everything in place to get started, but if you want to truly prosper and cultivate your core talent, you will need to do it legitimately.

As soon as you can, file proper business paperwork. Open a merchant account with your bank or use services like Stripe, Square, QuickBooks, PayPal, etc. Some people will use Zelle, Venmo, or CashApp. I'm not offering legal advice, but make sure that you have a way to collect your cash if you want to turn your talents into treasure.

Maybe you are in the startup phase, and you don't know where to begin. If you have identified your core talent by now, it'll be easier to become an official business. Doing something because you saw someone else doing it may not last for long and may cost you time and money!

If you're already established and doing something that drains the life out of you, you can decide to shift lanes. People like to say, "Stay in your lane." I always say, "Stay in your lane is aimed at those who choose to remain bound to the ground. There are no lanes in the sky when you fly!"

You can reinvent yourself today. You can rebrand. You can relaunch. Do not become stuck in something you cannot stand, even if it makes you money. It's worth it to enjoy making money by doing what you are naturally wired to do. So, let's identify that core talent and turn that talent into treasure.

Develop products, offer services, or both. Let the right people know that you are ready with the necessary solutions, services, or even entertainment. Don't allow what you decided years ago, your history, or the circumstances of life to block your economic borders. Act today!

I am turning my talents into treasure, and I am growing consistently. I hope that this helped you. I am Rekesha Pittman, and I am cultivating my core talent. Will you?

REKESHA PITTMAN

Rekesha Pittman excels at turning talents into treasure. She has helped visionaries worldwide launch profitable books and businesses through innovative training and strategic systems. She is the creator of **The EAST Formula™**. Rekesha is in-demand as a professional speaker and strategist for a wide variety of topics including profitable book publishing, training & development, and entrepreneurship.

Rekesha has authored multiple books including:

The EAST Formula
Entrepreneur | Author | Speaker | Trainer

Birth of a Saleswoman
Conquer Financial Failure. Create Financial Freedom.

ABCs of Authorship
Building Blocks for Emerging Authors

Book Publishing Master Plan
5 Fast Phases for Profitable Publishing

7 Ways to Get Speaking Engagements

Masterful Mentorship
Leadership, Life, and Love Lessons

Rekesha has professionally coached over 1,000 authors worldwide to publish bookstore-quality books. She provides innovative web-u-cation sessions, creative curriculum, strategic coaching, and proven profit-making strategies through innovative online training, speaking platforms, live workshops, masterminds, and group educational sessions.

Contact Information:

Website:
www.theEASTformula.com

Email:
theEASTformula@gmail.com

Social Media: **@RekeshaPittman**

EAST →

ENTREPRENEUR | AUTHOR | SPEAKER | TRAINER

THE EAST FORMULA

The most prominent entrepreneurs understand that implementing **The EAST Formula** is necessary to maximize influence and profits for influential impact. Running a business alone is not enough. Writing books without a defined strategy can lead to disaster. Speaking on stages without having books to continue the conversation means leaving money on the table. Launching training programs without significant reach can hamper profitability. All four components: **Entrepreneur, Author, Speaker,** and **Trainer** are winning strategies when implemented together for serial success. Go **EAST** and discover the formula for unlimited opportunity and innovative income streams.

ENTREPRENEUR

Explore passive and positive income opportunities that complement your personal passions and talents. Implement key systems and processes to grow your company and expand your reach.

AUTHOR

Develop an ideal book topic to enhance and foster paid speaking opportunities and training programs. Create lead magnets for customer acquisition and awareness. Create sales strategies and marketing campaigns.

SPEAKER

Review and develop existing and new signature topics for profitable speaking opportunities. Cultivate additional platforms and increase revenue streams during in-person and virtual appearances.

TRAINER

Create a series of training programs based on your book topic and signature talks. Establish training objectives, core demographics, curriculum, pricing, and delivery methods.

theEASTformula.com